Other books by Author

So You Want to Know the Secret of Starting a Business With Little or No Money
(Now available in Paper Back and Kindle)

So You Want To Open a Restaurant
This guide includes Spread Sheet Management Tools as well as information on lease negotiation, advertising, marketing and plating. It also includes or menu.
(Now available in Paper Back and Kindle)

So You Want To Open a Restaurant Expanded Addition
Includes both Recipes from the Kitchens of Cosmic Pizza and Simply Delicious Pizza and Recipes from the Kitchen of The Chocolate Martini in this book
(Now available in Paper Back and Kindle)

Recipes from the Kitchens of Cosmic Pizza and Simply Delicious Pizza
(Now available on Kindle and in Paper Back)

Recipes from the Kitchen of The Chocolate Martini Restaurant
(Now available on Kindle and in Paper Back)

Kefir, Probiotics & Your Health
(Now available on Kindle and in Paper Back)

From the Inside, Florida Divorce
(Now available on Kindle and in Paper Back)

Live Without Stress
(Now available on Kindle and in Paper Back)

About the Author

The author has owned Real Estate and Mortgage companies, 8 Restaurants, Legal Document companies, Marketing and Advertising companies, Fund Raising Consulting and Manufacturing companies as well as Holistic Schools and started them with little or No money

My Promise to YOU!

This book is dedicated to all of you who have taken the first step to owning their own business, having the desire and doing something about it!

Acknowledgment

I have always realized that when entering a new business arena there is someone or a few someone's that I needed to seek out to learn from. I needed a mentor or mentors!

In short - You must know when you're the Master and when you're the Student.

That is what I hope I can be for you, a Mentor!

Content

Basic Business Research

Analyzing Information

Work at Home Marketing

Rules, What Rules!

INTRODUCTION

This eBook is a way for us to give back something to society, to help others as we have been helped. Everyone needs help.

Think of this as a training center designed to help you open your own business, with little or no money.

These income producing businesses work, are easy to start at home in your spare time regardless of your educational background, limitations and with little or no money.

We've owned and operated many businesses in the past 40 to 45 years. Almost all of them were started with little or no money!

Mentoring Concept General Description

Part 1

Gives you a lot of background about myself and how I started, learned about business, grew and how I got to where I am today. This is more than ego; it's lessons on how to find your way.

My first book, "So You Want to Open a Restaurant", was obviously limited to the restaurant business but it gave a lot of background about how I ended up there so I'm going to use that same approach here to set up a thought process for you to use as we move forward to our ultimate goal, you starting a business with little or no money.

Some of you may have an idea as to what

you want to do already, which is great.

Perhaps just our marketing or money ideas will make the difference in your getting started sooner.

Please look at what I'm presenting as educational, mentoring and proven business practices.

The secret of opening a business, any business is being ready.

Sounds simple and it is!

To begin with a lot depends on how you think so we'll start there.

Part 2

Thinking "Outside the Box", starting with a Change of Attitude

Then we'll go over some of the many businesses that can be started with little or no money today.

Part 3

Here we do a little soul searching to see what we really what.

This process will guide you to discovering what will work for you, what questions to ask yourself during the process and finally how to get started.

ABOUT US

It is always difficult to tell people about yourself. After all we're talking about a 40 to 45 year period of business experiences. For the last 26 years Babette and I worked together almost every day.

So, to simplify things we are going to use a resume format to cover a lot of time periods a bit further on.

With that said I want everyone to realize that over the years we had successes as well as failures. We learned a lot from our failures! Yes, I said failures!

While I went to college for a few years prior to going into the Army I was really an APPRENTICE. I spent almost my entire youth working for my father at our family business. The business went public in 1959. Think of it as a department store with a heavy emphasis on office supplies and printing.

I worked from the stock rooms all the way up to helping open branch stores in Rockefeller Center in New York City and White Plains N.Y.

A great deal of the time I would sit in my father's office and just listen and observe the various meetings going on.

Sometimes I was prepped as to what to watch for and told what the other person was going to say and agree to. 9 out of 10 times my father was correct. It was very interesting lessons.

The men and woman who worked there had a high school education with a few collage educated people.

In those days your work experience was looked at first. Sure, education counted, second!

My first job after service was as an assistant to a President and Chairman of a public company that owned oil wells, banks, manufacturing facilities, cattle ranches, gravel business and farm stores. They taught me many things about business just as my father had. I learned a lot on the job every day.

The last public company I worked for was a mixture of manufacturing consumer products and mail and telemarketing to business and preparing fund raising packages for churches, schools, bands, sports teams and Boy scouts etc. I was the VP of Marketing.

While there I was looking for an outside sales person to help start a new retail division.

Personal, (now Human Resources), ran an employment ad that stated a college degree was needed to apply.

When I asked them why they put the college requirement in I was told "It kept the masses away".

I told them to remove the unnecessary college requirement. Shortly thereafter I found just the person I needed.

She received the same pay as a college grad because she had the experience I needed and was willing to apprentice, to learn what was needed. She did great and later she started her own sales firm.

What's ironic is that every company who hires has a way they expect things done so even a college graduate learns on the job, so the college education in many ways meant nothing, that's how it is! Remember this as we move forward as it is one of the secrets you need to know.

I want to make one last point about this company.

We had Monday morning meetings about different promotions and the creating of them.

At each and every meeting the 16 department or division heads would be asked questions by me and would turn to their assistants and ask them for the information which they would present.

This got me to think about why I had these people as division heads.

So the Friday following I had all the assistants meet me in my private office and asked them what I would have normally asked the next Monday meeting.
They of course had all the answers right at their fingertips. These questions were very basic and any division head should be able to answer them on the spot just as the assistants did.

I instructed them to come back to my

private office on Monday instead of going to the normal conference room and not to discuss anything about this meeting with anyone.

The next Monday was very interesting, not one of the 16 division heads could answer my questions and all stated they would get back to me.

Shortly thereafter I promoted all the assistants to replace the division heads.

I bring this story up to prove a point. When people are given a chance they can do amazing things. YOU can do amazing things!

You need to give yourself a chance and I'm going to pave the way for you.

Many times in my search for information about a niche or pin point market area I'd "get a job" so I could get hands on, "on the job training" from a company that was successful in that market. I wanted access so I could see and hear what they were doing. It didn't matter what the management job was or what it paid, I was there to learn.

I became an *Apprentice* and learned all I needed to open my own business.

So when I say you can do anything you want I mean it! You're as smart as I am, or anyone else, for that matter.

Believe in yourself and take the time to learn from others it will save you many hours of worry and self-doubts.

As you go through this book think of it as "On the Job" training getting you ready for your own business!

Here's both my Modified Resume and Babette's Modified Resume mentioned above;

Michael -

1969- Asst. to Pres. & Chairman Tiffany Inc.

1971- Macy's Asst. Buyer, Small Electrics, NY Herald Square NY

1972- Non- Food Product Development Manager Gerber Foods, HanksCraft Division

1973- Private Label Sales, Product Specialties div of Sunbeam

1975- Director of Marketing and Div. head of Specialty Products for Ketchum and McDougall

1978- VP Marketing Cadence Industries

1979- President and Partner of Financial Specialties

1980- President and Owner

Garfield and Asso., Business Builders- a fund raising company, Data Works- (a University Software Program and Installer Provider), Specialty Advertising- (Promotional Merchandise) Software Provider and factory representative.

Babette –
1983 through 1985-
Co-Owner of Marin Fish and Poultry

Babette and Michael, Owner Operators
1985 through 1996-
Gualala Realty and Mortgage, Point Arena
Laundromat, Capt.'s and owners of Essence-
a Salmon Trawler, The Human Touch School
of the Healing Arts, Simply Delicious Pizza,
Zarducci's, ABC Realty and Mortgage, ABC
Yacht Brokerage

1997 through 2004-
Garfield Realty, Florida Legal Document
Services, Cosmic Pizza. (Babette became a
selling Oil Painting Artist- The Cosmic
Gallery)

Babette and Michael-
2004 through 2007-
No Bad Days Inc., Realty Mexico, EBay Sales.

Babette and Michael

2007 to 2010-

Retired- (Sailing the Caribbean, Central and South America, Bocas Del Toro, Panama), Owners of Bocas Island Hideaway Resort, Owners- The Chocolate Martini Restaurant

Babette and Michael-

Nov 2010 to present-

Publishing, McKinney McCall Marketing, Mentors.

August 2014- Kefir World, marketers and manufacturers of "Making Kefir at Home Starter kits .

Mind Set for Success Part 1

All things start at the beginning so let's get to know your needs, strengths and wants.

Everything you do in your everyday life has a business component to it.

You identify what you need to do to reach a goal. You problem solve. You make budget choices. You act on your choices!

So, basically you're an executive. It doesn't matter if you were laid off, never had a job, are a Home Maker, Husband, Wife, Spouse Student, Disabled Vet, Vet, Active Military, Single Parent or Retired. You have skills, many skills that just need a little mentoring and focusing to discover them for what they are, an Executive Skill.

I'll bet you have hobbies and things you like to do with family and friends that have taught you more about business then you realize. Knowledge needed for the development of a business for necessary income or additional income.

The first part of developing your mind set has to do with EGO... Look let's be honest, we all want to be proud of ourselves and have people we love or respect to be proud of us.

It's great for an ego to say I'm the VP of a company and less so to say I'm in bug control or bookkeeping.

However, the VP is a line item in a budget and can be fired anytime. Your bug control or bookkeeping business is yours.

Here are 2 quick stories from my past to make my point.

As a teenager in Stamford Connecticut I meet our new neighbor and introduced him to my father. He was a garbage man and owned 2 trucks.

When he left I made an unkind comment about his business which prompted my father to straighten me out. He said simply that I maybe a President and major stock holder of a listed company but I'd rather be him any day of the week. He went on to explain as follows.

First I'd be my own boss without fear of problems from stockholders or the Board of Directors; you see I still can be fired.

Second, our neighbor is owner of the truck that collects our trash and I pay him to pick trash up 4 times a month. I pay $50 since we are not in the city proper. He has 15000 homes he collects from. That means he makes $750,000.00 every month. That's $9,000,000.00 a year. After expenses and taxes he still makes over $1,000,000.00.

My salary doesn't come close to that number. I definitely would rather be him!

However, while I never forgot this simple math lesson and "Forget titles, it's all about earning money". I missed the lessons message.

I wanted to be a big time Corporate Executive. I was stuck in "EGO".

What would others think of me instead of

what was best for me.

I went through this ego fight back in the early 70's when I was invited to join a business associate, Larry Ackers, in opening a sandwich shop in Naperville IL.

Family members really gave me a hard time and I passed on the opportunity because I didn't want to be known as a guy who owned a sandwich shop. Larry went on to build a very successful chain.
I instead went to work at a large manufacturing company as a marketing director.

When they closed the division I was again offered ownership of a sandwich shop but this time in New York City. The offer came from my step brother. Again I turned it down. Another mistake!

It was a good 16 years later that I went into the restaurant business and was very successful.

I should have checked my ego at the door a lot sooner.

Mind Set for Success Part 2

The second part of developing a mindset is to understand how we develop **"Dogma"**, "The absolute things we know to be true" or are they? Here's an example, (Sorry, I can't remember where I heard this or I'd give the person credit)

5 monkeys are in a cage.

In the middle of the cage is a stairway that leads to a piece of hanging fruit.

Every time a monkey starts up the stairs to get the fruit the other 4 monkeys are dowsed with very cold water until the monkey on the stairway comes down.

This happens a few times and then when any monkey heads for the stairway the other monkeys jump him and beat him up.

One of the original monkeys is replaced and the new monkey heads up the stairs and is immediately jumped by the other 4.
Over time all the monkeys are replaced but the behavior of beating up any monkey who starts up the stairs continues, even though the reason for the attacks are unknown to the current 5 monkeys!

You do many things for reasons long forgotten, they seem correct but you can't remember why you do it that way.

Now is the time to allow for a change of thinking, forget **"Dogma"**.

Your mind set should support your ego but do remember to follow your own heart, forget corporate titles and being a line item in a corporate budget.

Yes, you need to respect your spouse and family but it's about making money not titles. It's about making money for yourself and family not stockholders.

Leave "Dogma" at the door and allow yourself to think outside the box.
Think "Why Not" instead of "I can't". Then test your "Idea", (more on testing later).

Work At Home Income Advertising

Now let's talk openly about some of the many "Business Opportunities" out in the real world and Internet.

Some are real and many are not, however they all cost you money to find out about **"THE SECRET"**!

When you see one of these infomercials or long winded ads study them for ideas how to apply some of the thinking that's in them.

Take them apart line by line. Some of the offers use Affiliate marketing. As an example of what I'm referring to we will pretend you buy an e-Book, like this one about opening a business, and on every page there is a company named that will supply you with – a website, business cards, products to sell, a newsletter, a service to send emails to potential customer or supply the raw materials you need for a suggested product like making "Bath Salts".

In each case the support suggested is pointing you to someone who is "Affiliated" with the e-Book seller. If you buy anything suggested the e-Book seller makes money, a commission or affiliate fee.

This is not necessarily a bad thing; however I think you should be informed. We are NOT using "Affiliate Marketing" in this e-Book.

The information here is based on our experience and can be worth a great deal of money when developed properly. Take advantage of ideas, remember your goals!

WORKING at HOME

What a pleasure it is to work at home, but you must set aside focused time.

You have many things that are normal and routine in your life at home, but there are many distractions. So it is important to develop work space that allows you the privacy you need to think and do your business.

You must set aside the appropriate hours of the day to do the work you choose. It's that simple!

Make it a routine that you and your family can live with.

Please be realistic with time planning, it will make your life much easier.

Explore What You Know

Every day we do things and never see the potential of them becoming a business. Our focus is on traditional ways of making money.

Shortly, I'll show you a partial list of some of the things we've thought about, some things we've done, some things we helped others do and some things we studied and plan to do. Please add to this list based on your own thoughts and experiences.

There is a famous saying,

"With a formal education you can make a living. Self-education will make you a fortune"!

So let's self-educate.

Consider the following...

1. In recent years a research scientist, the real deal, invented and patented a water pistol and made millions from royalties.

2. Someone I know extremely well, (me), looked at a scale truck bank made by Ertyl

Toys and saw an Item that corporations could use as promotion or a fund raising item and ended up selling over a million of them to companies like Heinz, Nabisco and The Telephone Pioneers, (AT&T).

I had no money, just an idea and made my presentation to Ertyl for them to do billing, to work on a commission and the rest is history.

This is an example of an Erytl truck bank similar to the ones I sold in the mid 80's.

3. When I was a mortgage broker I did a friend a favor and took restaurant equipment as security on a loan instead of real estate.

I ended up with the equipment and used it to open our first restaurant. In the 12 years that we were restaurateurs we owned 8 successful restaurants.

I had no formal training, but I did train as an apprentice with the man I got the equipment from! (He is a friend to this day).

That's how our Simply Delicious Pizza chain got started. The other restaurants followed that.

4. I went through a divorce and after reviewing all the filed documents realized that they were forms!

I reviewed the family law forms in California, Florida and other states and discovered that anyone can fill out these forms for themselves, (Pro Se) or go to a legal document company and receive help in filling them in for filing with the county clerk's office.

I opened a legal document company and had marginal success because the public in general thought you HAD to use a lawyer.

To get some credentials I went to work in Monroe County Florida as a part of the court administration division and became their Pro Se Family Court Program Specialist and learned with "ON THE JOB" training how to fill out the forms.

I planned to open a national legal document services business in the near future but never did. That company was my Florida Legal Document Services, Inc.

One of my books available through Amazon is on getting a Florida Divorce.

5. A writer living in New York City needed to make some extra money since his writing wasn't going well. He started to grow Heirloom Tomatoes on his apartment roof. He marketed to upscale restaurants in New York City. He did so well that he bought land and became a big supplier of tomatoes to NY restaurants and then wrote a book about it. The book was published. He still sells tomatoes successfully as well.

6. A single woman went to a second hand close store and found they sold used, donated cloths and shoes for $1.00 a pound. She also saw that many items were new or floor samples as well as designer label cloths. She bought cloths at a $1.00 a pound and went to a local flea market to sell them and made a huge living and great business buying and reselling. What a great way to find things to sell.

In all **6** of these examples the individual made money with an idea outside his or her educational experience.

They took an idea, found a way to apprentice or get advice, mentoring and with work made their own success.

WE'RE GOING TO HELP YOU DO THIS TOO!

Believe in yourself!

Everything listed next has a business potential. YOU have many of these skills and anyone of them can be developed into a business.

Think about what I'm saying and study the list below, analysis it. Project the possible course you would take to develop one of these into a business. Be sure that what's on this list makes sense to you... not your friend, parents or spouse? Dream a little!

Don't be Sarah!

Sarah is a very smart woman I've known for over 30 years. She has had some of the best work at home business ideas I've ever heard of.

I can't tell you how many times I've listened to her and even offered to help bring her ideas to a successful conclusion. All to no avail even though she really needs a business income to help pay her bills and relieve stress from her life.

Here are some of her ideas...

Long before the likes of the Celestial Tea Company started she developed a Tea company. This was before I knew her.

Before it had a chance to grow she sold it. Why you ask, because she didn't know how to grow it and didn't know or look for a mentor to help her. She was stuck.

Stuck with fear of failure and stuck with fear of success. She didn't have proper support or knowledge just a great idea.

Years later she came to me and talked about a spice and seasoning business idea based on an herb mix she used when cooking as well as a salad dressing she used in her restaurant. (She bought one of mine and I was now her restaurant mentor).

As part of my suggestions I said why not test to see how the retailers and consumers felt about your products.

I made suggestions how to price out the products, how to do the test marketing and eventually how to mass produce the products.

Periodically I bring up the project and after many years of nothing happening I recently offered to do the pricing for her as well as lay out a test marketing program.

I hope she takes me up it, we'll see.

Wishing you want or need a business will not make it happen, only action will!

Only "YOU" can take action, DO IT!

Mind Set for Success Part 3

Work from Home Businesses

Computer Based sales businesses-

EBay, Craig's list

Affiliate Marketing

Cleaning

Bookkeeping

Lawn Care/Gardening

Cooking/Baking/Candy

Event Planning

Dog Walking/Pet Care

Baby Sitting, House sitting

Buying/Selling Books

Garage Sales

Fund Raising Programs and Products

Mystery Shopper

Estate Sales /Flea Mkts

Storage Auctions

Photography

Make Soap, Dried flower or herb Sashays

Music, Poetry and Writing

Arts and Crafts

Wood Working

Coin/Stamp Collecting

Pottery

Macramé

Sewing/Knitting/Quilting

Gardening/ herbs for sale
Growing veggies/ berries or fruit
Organic Potato/ Tomato
Growing Hops for hobby beer brewers

Buying bulk herbs and blending your own seasoning, curries, bath salt or teas for sale.

Now, add MORE right here, make a list!
1.
2.
3.
4.
5.
6.
7.
8.
9.
10.
Notes:

USING WHAT YOU KNOW

We're getting ready to move to your real world. You've had time to review the list I provided and add to it... things like making Bath Salts, Consulting, Decorating, Wood Working, Becoming a Hunting or Fishing Guide, etc.

Now how do we do something with your selection to make MONEY with little or NO money?

Hobbies to Business

I always like wood working and pottery but decided to make outdoor furniture based on the tools I had.

I looked up the New Yankee Workshop and found a design for an Adirondack chair #202. I made some and then went to a retail store that sold outdoor furniture.

The store owner ordered 4 chairs, $1000

worth. It took me many hours to make the order and I learned a wonderful lesson. Just because you can do it doesn't mean you can make money doing it.

The $1000 looks great but the cost of wood, paint, power tools and labor reduced my earnings greatly and a hobby became a pain. Moreover, the retailer just wanted to use the chairs as a road side draw to get people to stop and see the rest of his store.

I had made the chairs so that they looked like fish bones not just regular chairs.

If I felt this was a viable business I'd have tooled and purchased equipment to make the labor next to nothing, however I saw the market as a local market with a limited buying customer potential at the retail prices necessary. I also felt that cheap furniture would soon come out of China. I was right.

Here's a chair I made for family in California in 2002, the picture was taken in 2010. Looks good!

Basically I tested the market and found that it was limited.

What I'm saying is niche markets are great but you have to look at what the real potential is, what you can charge, who is the leader in the market and what do they charge. Can you compete and what will it cost to compete.

Thinking back I remembered another home business that could be started locally with little cost or no cost and could grow into a national business, managing "Fund Raising".

Business Builders Fund Raising Management Program

This business allowed me to help others, make money and still work from home with ease.

The company developed fundraising products, fund raising program creation and supported fund raising efforts by managing solicitations.

Basically I supplied product, programs and marketing support for groups who were doing fundraisers to provide something like uniforms or musical instruments or money that was needed at a school, house of worship, charity, boys and girls club, bands, sports teams, communities or for those who wished to help an individual or family who fell on hard times because of medical costs or even a death. I enjoyed helping others help themselves!

The fund raising business also allowed us to hire other local representatives to work as our representatives in the market places near and around those doing fundraising.

The people who become our representative were trained by us and worked with their communities from their homes. If and when they wanted they could go out on their own to develop their own business with our support or on their own with our blessing.

They worked their own hours, coordinate events with us or on their own.

One of the things you learn fast is that you

cannot do everything yourself, neither can people needing fund raising. They need support and you need support and that was what we provided to the outside sales representative and their clients or customers.

This type of business really needs little in the way of funds to start.

I keep a website, e-BusinessBuilders.com available if I choose to re-enter fundraising.

Think of it this way, every year you see people trying to raise funds for school activities or religious institutions, but they never store the information or re-contact donors. Because most events are headed by volunteers you could present a plan to help them manage the fund raising events for a percentage, or by supplying products for them to sell.

One of the examples I'd like you to look at is http://www.goatmilkstuff.com/Goat-Milk-Soap-Fundraiser.html. This family took what they had and developed fund raising products to help others. I've never seen this product before, so I think it's a winner.

Basic Business Research

I'm going to give you a simple plan that will drive your success regardless of what you select to do. I'm serious!

Ok, let's get to it! First...

Everything in business is about buying and selling.

Every business uses research, market plans, budgets, sales and cost projections.
While simple, these things take time to do right.

So be prepared to sit down with pen and paper to make notes about each business option you think are viable for you.

With the use of the Internet you can find many resources to help make your business plan a success.

Deciding what you want to do is going to be the hardest thing you do but here's a good guideline to use while you decide.

Guide Lines to be Considered

1. Who can use this service?

2. How many people or businesses can use this service in my work area?

3. Who provides this service now and how are they doing. Are they local?

4. What do I need to provide this service and to provide it better in some way other than price savings? (Price savings is good but people like something more).

Think about what I just asked. Pretty simple but if done right it's the foundation of your business. Be honest with yourself.

Call your competition and do research. Interview them as if you are a potential customer. Ask questions, prices, etc.

Observe how they're treating you, are they really answering your questions or putting you off for some reason.

6. How long have they been in business, what's their reputation?

If the questioning is right you will learn about how they market-

Is it in one step or more, (do they want to come by or do they get your telephone number and address to send more information)

What is their sales patter about themselves or the service or product they provide?

Is price their main benefit or is their quote based on the service they provide and the quality of their service.

You see simple questions can help you learn

a lot about a market and the businesses in them.

Now the hard part... Once you have this information your real work begins.

Analyzing Information

1. What would it cost you to provide this service or product? What is the actual cost?

As a very simple example if you are going to make a basic candle you will need wax, molds, wicks and heat. The total cost would be divided by the number of candles you can make with this material. 12 candle cost 12 dollars or a dollar per unit. If you retail the candles for $4 it's a 4 times mark up and profitable. That is if the current market price is the same or greater.

2. If you are providing a service like dog

walking then your cost is for dog treats, poop bags, marketing, business cards and a cell phone.

3. As a sales representative you work on commissions. Travel cost, cell phone and business cards are your cost.

4. If you're going to provide fund raising support then you'll need a phone, computer and a list of potential clients or customer and an idea of the type of fundraising taking place in your community.

5. Garage sales and Flea Market sales requires a source of items to be sold, storage, portable signage.

You get the idea!

Work At Home Income

Whatever you select will take some time to develop. Nothing usually happens fast. However this is a good thing!

Time allows you to correct any mistakes in ads, costs or marketing plan.

Here's an example- I was going to offer a small classified ad booklet where merchants paid for space. Additionally, we were going on Cable and Radio to advertise the pamphlet and send out copies to select communities. The total package was new for its time.

When I hired a sales rep we found that someone came through the area the year before with just a mailing piece. They took money but didn't perform. We had only made samples on our computer as well as a story board to show the Cable ads and a tape of the radio ad. The real cost was less than $100. Taking our time and testing the promotion saved us a lot of money! We would have failed if we did that program in that community.

When you develop a business you have a lot to learn regardless of your back ground. Each business start is unique!

Regardless of what you select to do as a business the hardest part is to market or tell people what you do and have them use your service. The first client or customer is the hardest to find.

While you may not realize it yet you have a network of friends, family, acquaintances and even strangers you can contact to help jump start your business.

However you first have to have a business plan to show them that you are serious.

You need something to present to them to show that you really are in business.

Methods used to SUPPORT your EFFORT

"Business Cards, Announcements, Website, Social Media Networking"!

An ANNOUNCEMENT can take many forms from an email, a flyer, a classified ad, a PR piece sent to the local Radio Station, Cable TV program, Posting on the many bulletin boards in restaurants and supermarkets and local businesses.

It should include what you do; the days and hours you do it, email address or cell number, a street address and some form of introductory information or savings.

The information should be fun, not dry like this. Let it reflect your personality and business style, be honest.

Licensing and Taxes

While I hate to bring it up we also have to look at what license or licensing we need to do business in a town, county or state.

Sorry, you can postpone it but you do need to deal with it as your business grows.

I promise that I'll lead you out of the weeds... please bear with me it will become very simple since I'm going to walk you through the whole process. What we are creating now is a foundation of thought.

Rules, What Rules... There is only one!

You always keep your word even if it means you'll lose money!

If you make a promise you need to keep it. So be careful what you promise.

If you promise a delivery will be made then plan for it to happen.
If for some reason you discover a problem contact your client and tell them right away.

Always be honest! However don't be a hero. That means you don't need to call your client if you think there might be a problem only if there is a problem.

An After Thought

Some of us are what the world calls "Entrepreneurs"; we just can't do the 8 to 5 thing.

We make the world interesting and when you have a spouse that supports you everything follows.

Every time we made a move or developed a new business we supported one another. I can stress how important it is that you support one another.

Do your planning together... If you are alone then you need to find someone to bounce ideas off of. Someone who will ask hard questions while still giving you support. Find a "Mentor" if you can.

If you can't email me and I'll do my level

best to help you find your path.

Mickeyg61@hotmail.com

www.ingramcontent.com/pod-product-compliance
Lightning Source LLC
Chambersburg PA
CBHW051248170526
45165CB00004B/1623